I WILL PRAY WITH THE SPIRIT

&

With the Understanding Also

or

A Discourse Touching Prayer

by

John Bunyan

Published by

Bible Truth Revealed & Eternal Realities

Copyright © 2015

First Published: 1663
Originally edited by George Offor

ISBN: 978-0-9941997-2-0

For more books & resources visit:

www.bibletruthrevealed.com
www.eternalrealities.com

Contents

Advertisement by the Editor...7
On Praying in the Spirit..10
First: What Prayer Is..11
Second: What it is to Pray with the Spirit.......................21
Third: What it is to Pray with the Spirit and with the Understanding..34
Fourth: Use and Application...45
The Conclusion..56
Footnotes..57

ADVERTISEMENT BY THE EDITOR

There is no subject of more solemn importance to human happiness than prayer. It is the only medium of intercourse with heaven. "It is that language wherein a creature holds correspondence with his Creator; and wherein the soul of a saint gets near to God, is entertained with great delight, and, as it were, dwells with his heavenly Father."[1] God, when manifest in the flesh, hath given us a solemn, sweeping declaration, embracing all prayer–private, social, and public–at all times and seasons, from the creation to the final consummation of all things–"God is a Spirit, and they that worship him *must worship him in Spirit and in truth*" (John 4:24).

The great enemy of souls, aided by the perverse state of the human mind, has exhausted his ingenuity and malice to prevent the exercise of this holy and delightful duty. His most successful effort has been to keep the soul in that fatal lethargy, or death unto holiness, and consequently unto prayer, into which it is plunged by Adam's transgression. Bunyan has some striking illustrations of Satan's devices to stifle prayer, in his history of the Holy War. When the troops of Emmanuel besiege Mansoul, their great effort was to gain "eargate" as a chief entrance to Mansoul, and at that important gate there were placed, by order of Diabolous, "the Lord Will-be-will, who made one old Mr. Prejudice, an angry and ill-conditioned fellow, captain of that ward, and put under his power sixty men called Deafmen to keep it," and these were arrayed in the most excellent armour of Diabolous, "*a dumb and prayerless spirit.*"

Nothing but the irresistible power of Emmanuel could have overcome these obstacles. He conquers and reigns supreme, and Mansoul becomes happy; prayer without ceasing enables the new-born man to breathe the celestial atmosphere. At length

Carnal Security interrupts and mars this happiness.

The Redeemer gradually withdraws.

Satan assaults the soul with armies of doubts, and, to prevent prayer, Diabolous "lands up Mouthgate with dirt."[2] Various efforts are made to send petitions, but the messengers make no impression, until, in the extremity of the soul's distress, two acceptable messengers are found, not dwelling in palaces, but in "a very mean cottage,"[3] their names were "Desires Awake and Wet Eyes," illustrating the inspired words, "Thus saith the High and lofty One that inhabiteth eternity, whose name is holy: I dwell–with him–that is of a contrite and humble spirit" (Isa 57:15). By this we are taught the utter worthlessness of depending upon the prayers of saints on earth, or the glorified spirits of heaven. Our own prayers alone are availing. Our own "Desires-awake" and "Wet-eyes," our own aspirations after God, our own deep repentance and sense of utter helplessness drives us to the Saviour, through whom *alone* we can find access and adoption into the family of our Father who is in heaven.

The soul that communes with God attains an aptitude in prayer which no human learning can give; devotional expressions become familiar; the Spirit of adoption leads them with deep solemnity to approach the Infinite Eternal as a father. Private prayer is so essentially spiritual that it cannot be reduced to writing. "A man that truly prays one prayer, shall after that never be able to express with his mouth, or pen the unutterable desires, sense, affection, and longing that went to God in that prayer". Prayer leads to "pure religion and undefiled," "to visit the fatherless and widows in their affliction," and to preserve us "unspotted from the world" (James 1:27). Blessed indeed are those who enjoy an abiding sense of the Divine presence; the Christian's divine life may be measured by his being able to "pray without ceasing," to "seek God's face continually." Men ought always to pray," and to "continue in prayer." This does not consist in perpetually repeating any form of prayer, but in that devotional frame of mind which enables the soul to say, "For me to live is Christ." When David was compassed about with the sorrows of hell, he at once ejaculates, "O Lord, I beseech thee deliver my soul." When the disciples were in danger they did not recite the Lord's Prayer, or any other form, but at once cried, "Lord, save us, we perish." Bunyan, speaking of private prayer, keenly inquires, will God not hear thee "except thou comest before him with some eloquent oration?" "It is not, as many take it to be, even a few babbling, prating, complimentary expressions, but a sensible feeling in the heart." Sincerity and a dependence upon the mediatorial office of Christ is all that God requires. "The Lord is nigh unto all them that call upon him–*in truth*" (Psa 145:18). In all that related to the individual approach of the spirit to its heavenly Father, our pious author offended not; but having enjoyed communion with God, he was, as all Christians are, desirous of communion with the saints on earth, and in choosing the forms of public worship, he gave great offence to many by rejecting the Book of Common Prayer.

To compel or to bribe persons to attend religious services is unjustifiable, and naturally produces hypocrisy and persecution. So it was with the decree of King Darius, (Dan 6); and so it has ever been with any royal or parliamentary interference with Christian liberty. "Who art thou that judgest another man's servant? to his own master he standeth or falleth" (Rom 14:4). "*every one* of us shall give account of himself to God" (Rom 14:12). All the solemnities of the day of judgment point not merely to the right, but to the necessity of private decision on all questions of faith, worship, and conduct, guided solely by the volume of inspiration. Mansoul, in its regenerate state, is the temple which the Creator has chosen for his worship; and it is infinitely more glorious than earthly edifices, which crumble into dust, while God's temples will be ever glorious as eternity rolls on.

Bunyan, to the sixteenth year of his age, had, when he attended public worship, listened to the Book of Common Prayer. At that time an Act of Parliament prohibited its use under severe and unjust penalties, and ordered the services to be conducted by the rules of a directory. In this an outline is given of public thanksgivings, confessions, and petitions; but no form of prayer. In the preface the Puritans record their opinion, that the Liturgy of the Church of England, notwithstanding all the pains and religious intentions of its compilers, hath proved an offence; unprofitable ceremonies hath occasioned much mischief; its estimation hath been raised by prelates, as if there were no other way of worship; making it an idol to the ignorant and superstitious, a matter of endless strife, and of increasing an idle ministry. Bunyan had weighed these observations, and recollected his former ignorance and superstition, when he counted all things holy connected with the outward forms, and did "very devoutly say and sing as others did."

But when he arose from the long and dread conflict with sin, and entered upon his Christian life, he decidedly preferred emancipation from forms of prayer, and treated them with great severity. He considered that the most essential qualification for the Christian ministry is the gift of prayer. Upon this subject learned and pious men have differed; but the opinions of one so eminently pious, and so well-taught in the Scriptures, are worthy of our careful investigation. Great allowances must be made for all that appears harsh in language, because urbanity was not the fashion of that day in religious controversy. He had been most cruelly imprisoned, with threats of transportation, and even an ignominious death, for refusing conformity to the Book of Common Prayer. Being conscientiously and prayerfully decided in his judgment, he set all these threats at defiance, and boldly, at the risk of his life, published this treatise, while yet a prisoner in Bedford jail; and it is a clear, concise, and scriptural discourse, setting forth his views upon this most important subject.

Any preconceived form would have fettered Bunyan's free spirit; he was a giant in prayer, and commanded the deepest reverence while leading the public devotions of the largest congregations. The great question as to public prayer is whether the minister should, relying upon Divine assistance, offer up prayer to God in the Saviour's name, immediately conceived under a sense of His presence; or whether it is better, as it is certainly easier, to read a form of prayer, from time to time, skillfully arranged, and with every regard to beauty of language? Which of these modes is most in accordance with the directions of the Sacred Scriptures, and most likely to be attended with spiritual benefit to the assembled church? Surely this inquiry does not involve the charge of schism or heresy upon either party.

"Let every man be fully persuaded in his own mind." Nor should such differences lead us to despise each other. Let our first inquiry be, whether the Saviour intended a fixed form of prayer? And if so, did he give His church any other than that most beautiful and comprehensive form called the Lord's Prayer? And did he license any one, and if so, who, to alter, add to, or diminish from it? On the other hand, should we conclude that "We know not what we should pray for as we ought, only as the Spirit helpeth our infirmities," then must we rely, as Bunyan did, upon the promised aid of that gracious Spirit. Blessed, indeed, are those whose intercourse with heaven sheds an influence on their whole conduct, gives them abundance of well-arranged words in praying with their families and with the sick or dejected, and–whose lives prove that they have been with Jesus, and are taught by him, or who, in Scripture language, "pray with the spirit and with the understanding also."

George Offor, 1692

ON PRAYING IN THE SPIRIT

"I will pray with the spirit, and I will pray with the understanding also."
1 Corinthians 14:15

Prayer is an *ordinance* of God, and that to be used both in public and private; yea, such an ordinance as brings those that have the spirit of supplication into great familiarity with God; and is also so prevalent in action, that it getteth of God, both for the person that prayeth, and for them that are prayed for, great things.[5] It is the opener of the heart of God, and a means by which the soul, though empty, is filled. By prayer the Christian can open his heart to God, as to a friend, and obtain fresh testimony of God's friendship to him. I might spend many words in distinguishing between public and private prayer; as also between that in the heart, and that with the vocal voice. Something also might be spoken to distinguish between the gifts and graces of prayer; but eschewing this method, my business shall be at this time only to show you the very heart of prayer, without which, all your lifting up, both of hands, and eyes, and voices, will be to no purpose at all. "I will pray with the Spirit."

The method that I shall go on in at this time shall be, FIRST. To show you what true prayer is. SECOND. To show you what it is to pray with the Spirit. THIRD. What it is to pray with the Spirit and understanding also. And so, FOURTHLY. To make some short use and application of what shall be spoken.

WHAT PRAYER IS

FIRST, What true prayer is. Prayer is a sincere, sensible, affectionate pouring out of the heart or soul to God, through Christ, in the strength and assistance of the Holy Spirit, for such things as God hath promised, or according to the Word, for the good of the church, with submission, in faith, to the will of God.

In this description are these seven things. First, It is a sincere; Second, A sensible; Third, An affectionate, pouring out of the soul to God, through Christ; Fourth, By the strength or assistance of the Spirit; Fifth, For such things as God hath promised, or, according to his word; Sixth, For the good of the church; Seventh, With submission in faith to the will of God.

First. For the first of these, it is a *sincere* pouring out of the soul to God. Sincerity is such a grace as runs through all the graces of God in us, and through all the actings of a Christian, and hath the sway in them too, or else their actings are not any thing regarded of God, and so of and in prayer, of which particularly David speaks, when he mentions prayer. "I cried unto him," the Lord "with my mouth, and he was extolled with my tongue. If I regard iniquity in my heart, the Lord will not hear" my prayer (Psa 66:17,18). Part of the exercise of prayer is sincerity, without which God looks not upon it as prayer in a good sense (Psa 16:1-4). Then "ye shall seek me and find me, when ye shall search for me with all your heart" (Jer 29:12-13). The want of this made the Lord reject their prayers in Hosea 7:14, where he saith, "They have not cried unto me with their heart," that is, in sincerity, "when they howled upon their beds." But for a pretence, for a show in hypocrisy, to be seen of men, and applauded for the same, they prayed. Sincerity was that which Christ commended in Nathaniel, when he was under the fig tree. "Behold, an Israelite indeed, in whom is no guile." Probably this good man was pouring out of his soul to God in prayer under the fig tree, and that in a sincere and unfeigned spirit before the Lord. The prayer that hath this in it as one of the principal ingredients, is the prayer that God looks at. Thus, "The prayer of the upright is his delight" (Prov 15:8).

And why must sincerity be one of the essentials of prayer which is accepted of God, but because sincerity carries the soul in all simplicity to open its heart to God, and to tell him the case plainly, without equivocation; to condemn itself plainly, without dissembling; to cry to God heartily, without complimenting. "I have surely heard Ephraim bemoaning himself thus; Thou has chastised me, and I was chastised, as a bullock unaccustomed to the yoke" (Jer 31:18). Sincerity is the same in a corner alone, as it is before the face of the world. It knows not how to wear two vizards, one for an appearance before men, and another for a short snatch in a corner; but it must have God, and be with him in the duty of prayer. It is not lip-labour that it doth regard, for it is the heart that God looks at, and that which sincerity looks at, and that which prayer comes from, if it be that prayer which is accompanied with sincerity.

Second. It is a sincere and *sensible* pouring out of the heart or soul. It is not, as many take it to be, even a few babbling, prating, complimentary expressions, but a sensible feeling there is in the heart. Prayer hath in it a sensibleness of diverse things; sometimes sense of sin, sometimes of mercy received, sometimes of the readiness of God to give mercy, &c.

1. A sense of the want of mercy, by reason of the danger of sin. The soul, I say, feels, and from feeling sighs, groans, and breaks at the heart. For right prayer bubbleth out of the heart when it is overpressed with grief and bitterness, as blood is forced out of the flesh by reason of some heavy burden that lieth upon it (1 Sam 1:10; Psa 69:3). David roars, cries, weeps, faints at heart, fails at the eyes, loseth his moisture, &c., (Psa 38:8-10). Hezekiah mourns like a dove (Isa 38:14). Ephraim bemoans himself (Jer 31:18). Peter weeps bitterly (Matt 26:75). Christ hath strong cryings and tears (Heb 5:7). And all this from a sense of the justice of God, the guilt of sin, the pains of hell and destruction. "The sorrows of death compassed me, and the pains of hell gat hold

upon me: I found trouble and sorrow." Then cried I unto the Lord (Psa 116:3,4). And in another place, "My sore ran in the night" (Psa 77:2). Again, "I am bowed down greatly; I go mourning all the day long" (Psa 38:6). In all these instances, and in hundreds more that might be named, you may see that prayer carrieth in it a sensible feeling disposition, and that first from a sense of sin.

2. Sometimes there is a sweet sense of mercy received; encouraging, comforting, strengthening, enlivening, enlightening mercy, &c. Thus David pours out his soul, to bless, and praise, and admire the great God for his loving-kindness to such poor vile wretches. "Bless the Lord, O my soul; and all that is within me bless his holy name. Bless the Lord, O my soul, and forget not all his benefits.[6] Who forgiveth all thine iniquities, who healeth all thy diseases; who redeemeth thy life from destruction; who crowneth thee with loving-kindness and tender mercies; who satisfieth thy mouth with good things, so that thy youth is renewed like the eagle's" (Psa 103:1-5). And thus is the prayer of saints sometimes turned into praise and thanksgiving, and yet are prayers still. This is a mystery; God's people pray with their praises, as it is written, "Be careful for nothing, but in every thing by prayer, and supplication, with thanksgiving, let your request be made known unto God" (Phil 4:6). A sensible thanksgiving, for mercies received, is a mighty prayer in the sight of God; it prevails with him unspeakably.

3. In prayer there is sometimes in the soul a sense of mercy to be received. This again sets the soul all on a flame. "Thou, O lord of hosts," saith David, "hast revealed to thy servant, saying I will build thee an house; therefore hath thy servant found in his heart to pray - unto thee" (2 Sam 7:27). This provoked Jacob, David, Daniel, with others–even a sense of mercies to be received–which caused them, not by fits and starts, nor yet in a foolish frothy way, to babble over a few words written in a paper; but mightily, fervently, and continually, to groan out their conditions before the Lord, as being sensible, sensible, I say, of their wants, their misery, and the willingness of God to show mercy (Gen 32:10,11; Dan 9:3,4).

A good sense of sin, and the wrath of God, with some encouragement from God to come unto him, is a better Common-prayer-book than that which is taken out of the Papistical mass-book,[7] being the scraps and fragments of the devices of some popes, some friars, and I wot not what.

Third. Prayer is a sincere, sensible, and an *affectionate* pouring out of the soul to God. O! the heat, strength, life, vigour, and affection, that is in right prayer! "As the hart panteth after the water-brooks, so panteth my soul after thee, O God" (Psa 42:1). "I have longed after thy precepts" (Psa 119:40). "I have longed for thy salvation" (ver 174). "My soul longeth, yea, even fainteth, for the courts of the Lord; my heart and my flesh crieth out for the living God" (Psa 84:2). "My soul breaketh for the longing that it hath unto thy judgments at all times" (Psa 119:20). Mark ye here, "My soul longeth," it longeth, it longeth, &c. O what affection is here discovered in prayer! The like you have in Daniel. "O Lord, hear; O Lord, forgive; O Lord, hearken and do; defer not, for thine own sake, O my God" (Dan 9:19). Every syllable carrieth a mighty vehemency in it. This is called the fervent, or the working prayer, by James. And so again, "And being in an agony, he prayed more earnestly" (Luke 22:44). Or had his affections more and more drawn out after God for his helping hand. O! How wide are the most of men with their prayers from this prayer, that is, *prayer* in God's account! Alas! The greatest part of men make no conscience at all of the duty; and as for them that do, it is to be feared that many of them are very great strangers to a sincere, sensible, and affectionate pouring out their hearts or souls to God; but even content themselves with a little lip-labour and bodily exercise, mumbling over a few imaginary prayers. When the affections are indeed engaged in prayer, then, then the whole man is engaged, and that in such sort, that the soul will spend itself to nothing, as it were, rather than it will go without that good desired, even communion and solace with Christ. And hence it is that the saints have spent their strengths, and lost their lives, rather than go without the blessing (Psa 69:3; 38:9,10; Gen 32:24,26).

All this is too, too evident by the ignorance, profaneness, and spirit of envy, that reign in the hearts of those men that are so hot for the forms, and not the power of praying. Scarce one of forty among them know what it is to be born again, to have communion with the Father through the Son; to feel the power of grace sanctifying their hearts: but for all their prayers, they still live cursed, drunken, whorish, and abominable lives, full of malice, envy, deceit, persecuting of the dear children of God. O what a dreadful after-clap is coming upon them! which all their hypocritical assembling themselves together, with all their prayers, shall never be able to help them against, or shelter them from.

Again, It is a pouring out of the heart or soul. There is in prayer an unbosoming of a man's self, an opening of the heart to God, an affectionate pouring out of the soul in requests, sighs, and groans. "All my desire is before thee," saith David, "and my groaning is not hid from thee" (Psa 38:9). And again, "My soul thirsteth for God, for the living God. When shall I come and appear before God? When I remember these things, I pour out my soul in me" (Psa 42:2,4). Mark, "I pour out my soul." It is an expression signifying, that in prayer there goeth the very life and whole strength to God. As in another place, "Trust in him at all times; ye people, - pour out your heart before him" (Psa 62:8). This is the prayer to which the promise is made, for the delivering of a poor creature out of captivity and thralldom. "If from thence thou shalt seek the Lord thy God, thou shalt find him, if thou seek him with all thy heart and with all thy soul" (Deut 4:29).

Again, It is a pouring out of the heart or soul *to God*. This showeth also the excellency of the spirit of prayer. It is the great God to which it retires. "When shall I come and appear before God?" And it argueth, that the soul that thus prayeth indeed, sees an emptiness in all things under heaven; that in God alone there is rest and satisfaction for the soul. "Now she that is a widow indeed, and desolate, trusteth in God" (1 Tim 5:5). So saith David, "In thee, O Lord, do I put my trust; let me never be put to confusion. Deliver me in thy righteousness, and cause me to escape; incline thine ear to me, and save me. Be thou my strong habitation, whereunto I may continually resort: - for thou art my rock and my fortress; deliver me, O my God, - out of the hand of the unrighteous and cruel man. For thou art my hope, O Lord God, thou art my trust from my youth" (Psa 71:1-5). Many in a wording way speak of God; but right prayer makes God his hope, stay, and all. Right prayer sees nothing substantial, and worth the looking after, but God. And that, as I said before, it doth in a sincere, sensible, and affectionate way.

Again, It is a sincere, sensible, affectionate pouring out of the heart or soul to God, *through Christ*. This through Christ must needs be added, or else it is to be questioned, whether it be prayer, though in appearance it be never so eminent or eloquent.

Christ is the way through whom the soul hath admittance to God, and without whom it is impossible that so much as one desire should come into the ears of the Lord of Sabaoth (John 14:6). "If ye shall ask anything in my name"; "whatsoever ye shall ask the Father in my name, I will do it" (John 14:13,14). This was Daniel's way in praying for the people of God; he did it in the name of Christ. "Now therefore, O our God, hear the prayer of thy servant, and his supplications, and cause thy face to shine upon thy sanctuary that is desolate, for the Lord's sake" (Dan 9:17). And so David, "For thy name's sake," that is, for thy Christ's sake, "pardon mine iniquity, for it is great" (Psa 25:11). But now, it is not every one that maketh mention of Christ's name in prayer, that doth indeed, and in truth, effectually pray to God in the name of Christ, or through him. This coming to God through Christ is the hardest part that is found in prayer. A man may more easily be sensible of his works, ay, and sincerely too desire mercy, and yet not be able to come to God by Christ. That man that comes to God by Christ, he must first have the knowledge of him; "for he that cometh to God, must believe that he is" (Heb 11:6). And so he that comes to God through Christ, must be enabled to know Christ. Lord, saith Moses, "show me now thy way, that I may know thee" (Exo 33:13).

This Christ, none but the Father can reveal (Matt 11:27). And to come through Christ, is for the soul to be enabled of God to shroud itself under the shadow of the Lord Jesus, as a man shroudeth himself under a thing for safeguard (Matt 16:16).[8] Hence it is that David so often terms Christ his shield, buckler, tower, fortress, rock of defence, &c., (Psa 18:2; 27:1; 28:1). Not only because by him he overcame his enemies, but because through him he found favour with God the Father. And so he saith to Abraham, "Fear not, I am thy shield," &c., (Gen 15:1). The man then that comes to God through Christ, must have faith, by which he puts on Christ, and in him appears before God. Now he that hath faith is born of God, born again, and so becomes one of the sons of God; by virtue of which he is joined to Christ, and made a member of him (John 3:5,7; 1:12). And therefore, secondly he, as a member of Christ, comes to God; I say, as a member of him, so that God looks on that man as a part of Christ, part of his body, flesh, and bones, united to him by election, conversion, illumination, the Spirit being conveyed into the heart of that poor man by God (Eph 5:30). So that now he comes to God in Christ's merits, in his blood, righteousness, victory, intercession, and so stands before him, being "accepted in his Beloved" (Eph 1:6). And because this poor creature is thus a member of the Lord Jesus, and under this consideration hath admittance to come to God; therefore, by virtue of this union also, is the Holy Spirit conveyed into him, whereby he is able to pour out himself, to wit, his soul, before God, with his audience. And this leads me to the next, or fourth particular.

Fourth. Prayer is a sincere, sensible, affectionate, pouring out of the heart or soul to God through Christ, by the strength or *assistance of the Spirit*. For these things do so depend one upon another, that it is impossible that it should be prayer, without there be a joint concurrence of them; for though it be never so famous, yet without these things, it is only such prayer as is rejected of God. For without a sincere, sensible, affectionate pouring out of the heart to God, it is but lip-labour; and if it be not through Christ, it falleth far short of ever sounding well in the ears of God. So also, if it be not in the strength and assistance of the Spirit, it is but like the sons of Aaron, offering with strange fire (Lev 10:1,2). But I shall speak more to this under the second head; and therefore in the meantime, that which is not petitioned through the teaching and assistance of the Spirit, it is not possible that it should be "according to the will of God (Rom 8:26,27).

Fifth. Prayer is a sincere, sensible, affectionate pouring out of the heart, or soul, to God, through Christ, in the strength and assistance of the Spirit, *for such things as God hath promised*, &c., (Matt 6:6-8). Prayer it is, when it is within the compass of God's Word; and it is blasphemy, or at best vain babbling, when the petition is beside the book. David therefore still in his prayer kept his eye on the Word of God. "My soul," saith he, "cleaveth to the dust; quicken me according to thy word." And again, "My soul melteth for heaviness, strengthen thou me according unto thy word" (Psa 119:25-28; see also 41, 42, 58, 65, 74, 81, 82, 107, 147, 154, 169, 170). And, "remember thy word unto thy servant, upon which thou hast caused me to hope" (ver 49). And indeed the Holy Ghost doth not immediately quicken and stir up the heart of the Christian without, but by, with, and through the Word, by bringing that to the heart, and by opening of that, whereby the man is provoked to go to the Lord, and to tell him how it is with him, and also to argue, and supplicate, according to the Word; thus it was with Daniel, that mighty prophet of the Lord. He understanding by books that the captivity of the children of Israel was hard at an end; then, according unto that word, he maketh his prayer to God. "I Daniel," saith he, "understood by books," viz., the writings of Jeremiah, "the number of the years whereof the word of the Lord came to Jeremiah, - that he would accomplish seventy years in the desolations of Jerusalem. And I set my face to the Lord God, to seek by prayer and supplications, with fasting, and sackcloth, and ashes" (Dan 9:2,3). So that I say, as the Spirit is the helper and the governor of the soul, when it prayeth according to the will of God; so it guideth by and according to, the Word of God and his promise. Hence it is that our Lord Jesus Christ himself did make a stop, although his life lay at stake for it. I could now pray to my Father, and he should give me more than twelve legions of angels; but how then must the scripture be fulfilled that thus it must be? (Matt 26:53,54). As who should say, Were there but a word for it in the scripture, I should soon be out of the hands of mine enemies, I should be helped by angels; but the scripture will not warrant this kind of praying, for that saith otherwise. It is a praying then according to the Word and promise. The Spirit by the Word must direct, as well in the manner, as in the matter of prayer. "I will pray with the Spirit, and I will pray with the understanding also" (1 Cor 14:15). But there is no understanding without the Word. For if they reject the word of the Lord, "what wisdom is in them?" (Jer 8:9).

Sixth. *For the good of the church.* This clause reacheth in whatsoever tendeth either to the honour of God, Christ's advancement, or his people's benefit. For God, and Christ, and his people are so linked together that if the good of the one be prayed for, to wit, the church, the glory of God, and advancement of Christ, must needs be included. For as Christ is in the Father, so the saints are in Christ; and he that toucheth the saints, toucheth the apple of God's eye; and therefore pray for the peace of Jerusalem, and you pray for all that is required of you. For Jerusalem will never be in perfect peace until she be in heaven; and there is nothing that Christ doth more desire than to have her there. That also is the place that God through Christ hath given to her. He then that prayeth for the peace and good of Zion, or the church, doth ask that in prayer which Christ hath purchased with his blood; and also that which the Father hath given to him as the price thereof. Now he that prayeth for this, must pray for abundance of grace for the church, for help against all its temptations; that God would let nothing be too hard for it; and that all things might work together for its good, that God would keep them blameless and harmless, the sons of God, to his glory, in the midst of a crooked and perverse nation. And this is the substance of Christ's own prayer in John 17. And all Paul's prayers did run that way, as one of his prayers doth eminently show. "And this I pray, that your love may abound yet more and more in knowledge, and in all judgment; that ye may approve things that are excellent; that ye may be sincere, and without offence, till the day of Christ. Being filled with the fruits of righteousness, which are by Jesus Christ unto the glory and praise of God" (Phil 1:9-11). But a short prayer, you see, and yet full of good desires for the church, from the beginning to the end; that it may stand and go on, and that in the most excellent frame of spirit, even without blame, sincere, and without offence, until the day of Christ, let its temptations or persecutions be what they will (Eph 1:16-21; 3:14-19; Col 1:9- 13).

Seventh. And because, as I said, prayer doth *submit to the will of God*, and say, Thy will be done, as Christ hath taught us (Matt 6:10); therefore the people of the Lord in humility are to lay themselves and their prayers, and all that they have, at the foot of their God, to be disposed of by him as he in his heavenly wisdom seeth best. Yet not doubting but God will answer the desire of his people that way that shall be most for their advantage and his glory. When the saints therefore do pray with submission to the will of God, it doth not argue that they are to doubt or question God's love and kindness to them. But because they at all times are not so wise, but that sometimes Satan may get that advantage of them, as to tempt them to pray for that which, if they had it, would neither prove to God's glory nor his people's good. "Yet this is the confidence that we have in him, that if we ask anything according to his will, he heareth us; and if we know that he hear us, whatsoever we ask, we know that we have the petitions that we desired of him," that is, we asking in the Spirit of grace and supplication (1 John 5:14,15). For, as I said before, that petition that is not put up in and through the Spirit, it is not to be answered, because it is beside the will of God. For the Spirit only knoweth that, and so consequently knoweth how to pray according to that will of God. "For what man knoweth the things of a man, save the spirit of man which is in him? even so the things of God knoweth no man but the Spirit of God" (1 Cor 2:11). But more of this hereafter. Thus you see, first, what prayer is. Now to proceed.

WHAT IT IS TO PRAY WITH THE SPIRIT

SECOND. I will pray with the Spirit. Now to pray with the Spirit–for that is the praying man, and none else, so as to be accepted of God–it is for a man, as aforesaid, sincerely and sensibly, with affection, to come to God through Christ, &c.; which sincere, sensible, and affectionate coming must be by the working of God's Spirit.

There is no man nor church in the world that can come to God in prayer, but by the assistance of the Holy Spirit. "For through Christ we all have access by one Spirit unto the Father" (Eph 2:18). Wherefore Paul saith, "For we know not what we should pray for as we ought; but the Spirit itself maketh intercession for us with groanings which cannot be uttered. And he that searcheth the hearts, knoweth what is the mind of the Spirit, because he maketh intercession for the saints according to the will of God" (Rom 8:26,27). And because there is in this scripture so full a discovery of the spirit of prayer, and of man's inability to pray without it; therefore I shall in a few words comment upon it.

"For we." Consider first the person speaking, even Paul, and, in his person, all the apostles. We apostles, we extraordinary officers, the wise master-builders, that have some of us been caught up into paradise (Rom 15:16; I Cor 3:10; II Cor 12:4). "We know not what we should pray for." Surely there is no man but will confess, that Paul and his companions were as able to have done any work for God, as any pope or proud prelate in the church of Rome, and could as well have made a Common Prayer Book as those who at first composed this; as being not a whit behind them either in grace or gifts.[9]

"For we know not what we should pray for." We know not the matter of the things for which we should pray, neither the object to whom we pray, nor the medium by or through whom we pray;

none of these things know we, but by the help and assistance of the Spirit. Should we pray for communion with God through Christ? should we pray for faith, for justification by grace, and a truly sanctified heart? none of these things know we. "For what man knoweth the things of a man, save the spirit of man which is in him? even so the things of God knoweth no man, but the Spirit of God" (1 Cor 2:11). But here, alas! the apostles speak of inward and spiritual things, which the world knows not (Isa 29:11).

Again, as they know not the matter, &c., of prayer, without the help of the Spirit; so neither know they the manner thereof without the same; and therefore he adds, "We know not what we should pray for as we ought"; but the Spirit helpeth our infirmities, with sighs and groans which cannot be uttered. Mark here, they could not so well and so fully come off in the manner of performing this duty, as these in our days think they can.

The apostles, when they were at the best, yea, when the Holy Ghost assisted them, yet then they were fain to come off with sighs and groans, falling short of expressing their mind, but with sighs and groans which cannot be uttered.

But here now, the wise men of our days are so well skilled as that they have both the manner and matter of their prayers at their finger-ends; setting such a prayer for such a day, and that twenty years before it comes. One for Christmas, another for Easter, and six days after that. They have also bounded how many syllables must be said in every one of them at their public exercises. For each saint's day, also, they have them ready for the generations yet unborn to say. They can tell you, also, when you shall kneel, when you shall stand, when you should abide in your seats, when you should go up into the chancel, and what you should do when you come there. All which the apostles came short of, as not being able to compose so profound a manner; and that for this reason included in this scripture, because the fear of God tied them to pray as they ought.

"For we know not what we should pray for as we ought." Mark this, "as we ought." For the not thinking of this word, or at least the not understanding it in the spirit and truth of it, hath occasioned these men to devise, as Jeroboam did, another way of worship, both for matter and manner, than is revealed in the Word of God (1 Kings 12:26-33). But, saith Paul, we must pray as we ought; and this WE cannot do by all the art, skill, and cunning device of men or angels. " For we know not what we should pray for as we ought, but the Spirit"; nay, further, it must be "the Spirit *itself*" that helpeth our infirmities; not the Spirit and man's lusts; what man of his own brain may imagine and devise, is one thing, and what they are commanded, and ought to do, is another. Many ask and have not, because they ask amiss; and so are never the nearer the enjoying of those things they petition for (James 4:3). It is not to pray at random that will put off God, or cause him to answer. While prayer is making, God is searching the heart, to see from what root and spirit it doth arise (1 John 5:14). "And he that searcheth the heart knoweth," that is, approveth only, the meaning "of the Spirit, because he maketh intercession for the saints according to the will of God." For in that which is according to his will only, he heareth us, and in nothing else. And it is the Spirit only that can teach us so to ask; it only being able to search out all things, even the deep things of God. Without which Spirit, though we had a thousand Common Prayer Books, yet we know not what we should pray for as we ought, being accompanied with those infirmities that make us absolutely incapable of such a work. Which infirmities, although it is a hard thing to name them all, yet some of them are these that follow.

First. Without the Spirit man is so infirm that he cannot, with all other means whatsoever, be enabled to think one right saving thought of God, of Christ, or of his blessed things; and therefore he saith of the wicked, "God is not in all his thoughts," (Psa 10:4); unless it be that they imagine him altogether such a one as themselves (Psa 50:21). For "every imagination of the thoughts of his heart was only evil," and that "continually" (Gen 6:5; 8:21). They then not being able to conceive aright of God to whom they pray, of Christ through whom they pray, nor of the things for which they pray, as is before showed, how shall they be able to address themselves to God, without the Spirit help this infirmity? Peradventure you will say, By the help of the Common Prayer Book;

but that cannot do it, unless it can open the eyes, and reveal to the soul all these things before touched. Which that it cannot, it is evident; because that is the work of the Spirit only. The Spirit itself is the revealer of these things to poor souls, and that which doth give us to understand them; wherefore Christ tells his disciples, when he promised to send the Spirit, the Comforter, "He shall take of mine and show unto you"; as if he had said, I know you are naturally dark and ignorant as to the understanding any of my things; though ye try this course and the other, yet your ignorance will still remain, the veil is spread over your heart, and there is none can take away the same, nor give you spiritual understanding but the Spirit. The Common Prayer Book will not do it, neither can any man expect that it should be instrumental that way, it being none of God's ordinances; but a thing since the Scriptures were written, patched together one piece at one time, and another at another; a mere human invention and institution, which God is so far from owning of, that he expressly forbids it, with any other such like, and that by manifold sayings in his most holy and blessed Word. (See Mark 7:7,8, and Col 2:16-23; Deut 12:30- 32; Prov 30:6; Deut 4:2; Rev 22:18). For right prayer must, as well in the outward part of it, in the outward expression, as in the inward intention, come from what the soul doth apprehend in the light of the Spirit; otherwise it is condemned as vain and an abomination, because the heart and tongue do not go along jointly in the same, neither indeed can they, unless the Spirit help our infirmities (Mark 7; Prov 28:9; Isa 29:13). And this David knew full well, which did make him cry, "Lord, open thou my lips, and my mouth shall show forth thy praise" (Psa 51:15). I suppose there is none can imagine but that David could speak and express himself as well as others, nay, as any in our generation, as is clearly manifested by his word and his works. Nevertheless when this good man, this prophet, comes into God's worship, then the Lord must help, or he can do nothing. "Lord, open thou my lips, and" then "my mouth shall show forth thy praise." He could not speak one right word, except the Spirit itself gave utterance. "For we know not what we should pray for as we ought, but the Spirit itself helpeth our infirmities." But,

Second. It must be a praying with the Spirit, that is, the effectual praying; because without that, as men are senseless, so hypocritical, cold, and unseemly in their prayers; and so they, with their prayers, are both rendered abominable to God (Matt 23:14; Mark 12:40; Luke 18:11, 12; Isa 58:2, 3). It is not the excellency of the voice, nor the seeming affection, and earnestness of him that prayeth, that is anything regarded of God without it. For man, as man, is so full of all manner of wickedness, that as he cannot keep a word, or thought, so much less a piece of prayer clean, and acceptable to God through Christ; and for this cause the Pharisees, with their prayers, were rejected. No question but they were excellently able to express themselves in words, and also for length of time, too, they were very notable; but they had not the Spirit of Jesus Christ to help them, and therefore they did what they did with their infirmities or weaknesses only, and so fell short of a sincere, sensible, affectionate pouring out of their souls to God, through the strength of the Spirit. That is the prayer that goeth to heaven, that is sent thither in the strength of the Spirit. For,

Third. Nothing but the Spirit can show a man clearly his misery by nature, and so put a man into a posture of prayer. Talk is but talk, as we use to say, and so it is but mouth- worship, if there be not a sense of misery, and that effectually too. O the cursed hypocrisy that is in most hearts, and that accompanieth many thousands of praying men that would be so looked upon in this day, and all for want of a sense of their misery! But now the Spirit, that will sweetly show the soul its misery, where it is, and what is like to become of it, also the intolerableness of that condition. For it is the Spirit that doth effectually convince of sin and misery, without the Lord Jesus, and so puts the soul into a sweet, sensible, affectionate way of praying to God according to his word (John 16:7-9).

Fourth. If men did see their sins, yet without the help of the Spirit they would not pray. For they would run away from God, with Cain and Judas, and utterly despair of mercy, were it not for the Spirit. When a man is indeed sensible of his sin, and God's curse, then it is a hard thing to persuade him to pray; for, saith his heart, "There is no hope," it is in vain to seek God (Jer 2:25;

18:12). I am so vile, so wretched, and so cursed a creature, that I shall never be regarded! Now here comes the Spirit, and stayeth the soul, helpeth it to hold up its face to God, by letting into the heart some small sense of mercy to encourage it to go to God, and hence it is called "the Comforter" (John 14:26).

Fifth. It must be in or with the Spirit; for without that no man can know how he should come to God the right way. Men may easily say they come to God in his Son: but it is the hardest thing of a thousand to come to God aright and in his own way, without the Spirit. It is "the Spirit" that "searcheth all things, yea, the deep things of God" (1 Cor 2:10). It is the Spirit that must show us the way of coming to God, and also what there is in God that makes him desirable: "I pray thee," saith Moses, "show me now thy way, that I may know thee" (Exo 33:13). And, He shall take of mine, and "show it unto you" (John 16:14).

Sixth. Because without the Spirit, though a man did see his misery, and also the way to come to God; yet he would never be able to claim a share in either God, Christ, or mercy, with God's approbation. O how great a task is it, for a poor soul that becomes sensible of sin and the wrath of God, to say in faith, but this one word, "Father!" I tell you, however hypocrites think, yet the Christian that is so indeed finds all the difficulty in this very thing, it cannot say God is its Father. O! saith he, I dare not call him Father; and hence it is that the Spirit must be sent into the hearts of God's people for this very thing, to cry Father: it being too great a work for any man to do knowingly and believingly without it (Gal 4:6). When I say knowingly, I mean, knowing what it is to be a child of God, and to be born again. And when I say believingly, I mean, for the soul to believe, and that from good experience, that the work of grace is wrought in him. This is the right calling of God Father; and not as many do, to say in a babbling way, the Lord's prayer (so called) by heart, as it lieth in the words of the book. No, here is the life of prayer, when in or with the Spirit, a man being made sensible of sin, and how to come to the Lord for mercy; he comes, I say, in the strength of the Spirit, and crieth Father. That one word spoken in faith, is better than a thousand prayers, as men call them, written and read, in a formal, cold, lukewarm way. O how far short are those people of being sensible of this, who count it enough to teach themselves and children to say the Lord's prayer, the creed, with other sayings; when, as God knows, they are senseless of themselves, their misery, or what it is to be brought to God through Christ! Ah, poor soul! Study your misery, and cry to God to show you your confused blindness and ignorance, before you be so rife in calling God your Father, or teaching your children either so to say. And know, that to say God is your Father, in a way of prayer or conference, without any experiment of the work of grace on your souls, it is to say you are Jews and are not, and so to lie. You say, Our Father; God saith, You blaspheme! You say you are Jew, that is, true Christians; God saith, You lie!

"Behold I will make them of the synagogue of Satan, which say they are Jews, and are not, but do lie" (Rev 3:9). "And I know the blasphemy of them that say they are Jews, and are not, but are the synagogue of Satan" (Rev 2:9). And so much the greater the sin is, by how much the more the sinner boasts it with a pretended sanctity, as the Jews did to Christ, in the 8th of John, which made Christ, even in plain terms, to tell them their doom, for all their hypocritical pretences (John 8:41-45). And yet forsooth every cursed whoremaster, thief, and drunkard, swearer, and perjured person; they that have not only been such in times past, but are even so still: these I say, by some must be counted the only honest men, and all because with their blasphemous throats, and hypocritical hearts, they will come to church, and say, "Our Father!" Nay further, these men, though every time they say to God, Our Father, do most abominably blaspheme, yet they must be compelled thus to do. And because others that are of more sober principles, scruple the truth of such vain traditions; therefore they must be looked upon to be the only enemies of God and the nation: when as it is their own cursed superstition that doth set the great God against them, and cause him to count them for his enemies (Isa 53:10). And yet just like to Bonner, that blood-red persecutor, they commend, I say, these wretches, although never so vile, if they close in with their traditions, to be good churchmen, the honest subjects; while God's people are, as it hath always been, looked upon to be a turbulent, seditious, and factious people (Ezra 4:12-16).

Therefore give me leave a little to reason with thee, thou poor, blind, ignorant sot.

(1.) It may be thy great prayer is to say, "Our Father which art in heaven," &c. Dost thou know the meaning of the very first words of this prayer? Canst thou indeed, with the rest of the saints, cry, Our Father? Art thou truly born again? Hast thou received the spirit of adoption? Dost thou see thyself in Christ, and canst thou come to God as a member of him? Or art thou ignorant of these things, and yet darest thou say, Our Father? Is not the devil thy father? (John 8:44). And dost thou not do the deeds of the flesh? And yet darest thou say to God, Our Father? Nay, art thou not a desperate persecutor of the children of God? Hast thou not cursed them in thine heart many a time? And yet dost thou out of thy blasphemous throat suffer these words to come, even our Father? He is their Father whom thou hatest and persecutest. But as the devil presented himself amongst the sons of God, (Job 1), when they were to present themselves before the Father, even our Father, so is it now; because the saints were commanded to say, Our Father, therefore all the blind ignorant rabble in the world, they must also use the same words, Our Father.

(2.) And dost thou indeed say, "Hallowed be thy name" with thy heart? Dost thou study, by all honest and lawful ways, to advance the name, holiness, and majesty of God? Doth thy heart and conversation agree with this passage? Dost thou strive to imitate Christ in all the works of righteousness, which God doth command of thee, and prompt thee forward to? It is so, if thou be one that can truly with God's allowance cry, "Our Father." Or is it not the least of thy thoughts all the day? And dost thou not clearly make it appear, that thou art a cursed hypocrite, by condemning that with thy daily practice, which thou pretendest in thy praying with thy dissembling tongue?

(3.) Wouldst thou have the kingdom of God come indeed, and also his will to be done in earth as it is in heaven? Nay, notwithstanding, thou according to the form, sayest, Thy kingdom come, yet would it not make thee ready to run mad, to hear the trumpet sound, to see the dead arise, and thyself just now to go and appear before God, to reckon for all the deeds thou hast done in the body? Nay, are not the very thoughts of it altogether displeasing to thee? And if God's will should be done on earth as it is in heaven, must it not be thy ruin? There is never a rebel in heaven against God, and if he should so deal on earth, must it not whirl thee down to hell? And so of the rest of the petitions. Ah! How sadly would even those men look, and with what terror would they walk up and down the world, if they did but know the lying and blaspheming that proceedeth out of their mouth, even in their most pretended sanctity? The Lord awaken you, and teach you, poor souls, in all humility, to take heed that you be not rash and unadvised with your heart, and much more with your mouth! When you appear before God, as the wise man saith, "Be not rash with thy mouth, and let not thine heart be hasty to utter any thing, (Eccl 5:2); especially to call God Father, without some blessed experience when thou comest before God. But I pass this.

Seventh. It must be a praying with the Spirit if it be accepted, because there is nothing but the Spirit that can lift up the soul or heart to God in prayer: "The preparations of the heart in man, and the answer of the tongue, is from the Lord" (Prov 16:1). That is, in every work for God, and especially in prayer, if the heart run with the tongue, it must be prepared by the Spirit of God. Indeed the tongue is very apt, of itself, to run without either fear or wisdom: but when it is the answer of the heart, and that such a heart as is prepared by the Spirit of God, then it speaks so as God commands and doth desire.

They are mighty words of David, where he saith, that he lifteth his heart and his soul to God (Psa 25:1). It is a great work for any man without the strength of the Spirit, and therefore I conceive that this is one of the great reasons why the Spirit of God is called a Spirit of supplications, (Zech 12:10), because it is that which helpeth the heart when it supplicates indeed to do it; and therefore saith Paul, "Praying with all prayer and supplication in the Spirit" (Eph 6:18). And so in my text, "I will pray with the Spirit." Prayer, without the heart be in it, is like a sound without life; and a heart, without it be lifted up of the Spirit, will never pray to God.

Eighth. As the heart must be lifted up by the Spirit, if it pray aright, so also it must be held up by the Spirit when it is up, if it continue to pray aright. I do not know what, or how it is with others' hearts, whether they be lifted up by the Spirit of God, and so continued, or no: but this I am sure of, First, That it is impossible that all the prayer-books that men have made in the world, should lift up, or prepare the heart; that is the work of the great God himself. And, in the second place, I am sure that they are as far from keeping it up, when it is up. And indeed here is the life of prayer, to have the heart kept with God in the duty. It was a great matter for Moses to keep his hands lifted up to God in prayer; but how much more then to keep the heart in it! (Exo 17:12).

The want of this is that which God complains of; that they draw nigh to him with their mouth, and honour him with their lips, but their hearts were far from him (Isa 29:13; Eze 33), but chiefly that they walk after the commandments and traditions of men, as the scope of Matthew 15:8, 9 doth testify. And verily, may I but speak my own experience, and from that tell you the difficulty of praying to God as I ought, it is enough to make your poor, blind, carnal men to entertain strange thoughts of me. For, as for my heart, when I go to pray, I find it so loth to go to God, and when it is with him, so loth to stay with him, that many times I am forced in my prayers, first to beg of God that he would take mine heart, and set it on himself in Christ, and when it is there, that he would keep it there. Nay, many times I know not what to pray for, I am so blind, nor how to pray, I am so ignorant; only, blessed be grace, the Spirit helps our infirmities (Psa 86:11).

O! the starting-holes that the heart hath in the time of prayer; none knows how many bye-ways the heart hath, and back- lanes, to slip away from the presence of God. How much pride also, if enabled with expressions. How much hypocrisy, if before others. And how little conscience is there made of prayer between God and the soul in secret, unless the Spirit of supplication be there to help? When the Spirit gets into the heart, then there is prayer indeed, and not till then.

Ninth. The soul that doth rightly pray, it must be in and with the help and strength of the Spirit; because it is impossible that a man should express himself in prayer without it. When I say, it is impossible for a man to express himself in prayer without it, I mean, that it is impossible that the heart, in a sincere and sensible affectionate way, should pour out itself before God, with those groans and sighs that come from a truly praying heart, without the assistance of the Spirit. It is not the mouth that is the main thing to be looked at in prayer, but whether the heart is so full of affection and earnestness in prayer with God, that it is impossible to express their sense and desire; for then a man desires indeed, when his desires are so strong, many, and mighty, that all the words, tears, and groans that can come from the heart, cannot utter them: "The Spirit — helpeth our infirmities, - and maketh intercession for us with [sighs and] groanings which cannot be uttered" (Rom 8:26).

That is but poor prayer which is only discovered in so many words. A man that truly prays one prayer, shall after that never be able to express with his mouth or pen the unutterable desires, sense, affection, and longing that went to God in that prayer.

The best prayers have often more groans than words: and those words that it hath are but a lean and shallow representation of the heart, life, and spirit of that prayer. You do not find any words of prayer, that we read of, come out of the mouth of Moses, when he was going out of Egypt, and was followed by Pharaoh, and yet he made heaven ring again with his cry (Exo 14:15). But it was inexpressible and unsearchable groans and cryings of his soul in and with the Spirit. God is the God of spirits, and his eyes look further than at the outside of any duty whatsoever (Num 16:22). I doubt this is but little thought on by the most of them that would be looked upon as a praying people (1 Sam 16:7).

The nearer a man comes in any work that God commands him to the doing of it according to his will, so much the more hard and difficult it is; and the reason is, because man, as man, is not able to do it. But prayer, as aforesaid, is not only a duty, but one of the most eminent duties, and therefore so much the more difficult: therefore Paul knew what he said, when he said, "I will pray with the Spirit." He knew well it was not what others writ or said that could make him a praying person; nothing less than the Spirit could do it.

Tenth. It must be with the Spirit, or else as there will be a failing in the act itself, so there will be a failing, yea, a fainting, in the prosecution of the work. Prayer is an ordinance of God, that must continue with a soul so long as it is on this side glory. But, as I said before, it is not possible for a man to get up his heart to God in prayer; so it is as difficult to keep it there, without the assistance of the Spirit. And if so, then for a man to continue from time to time in prayer with God, it must of necessity be with the Spirit.

Christ tells us, that men ought always to pray, and not to faint (Luke 18:1). And again tells us, that this is one definition of a hypocrite, that either he will not continue in prayer, or else if he do it, it will not be in the power, that is, in the spirit of prayer, but in the form, for a pretence only (Job 27:10; Matt 23:14). It is the easiest thing of a hundred to fall from the power to the form, but it is the hardest thing of many to keep in the life, spirit, and power of any one duty, especially prayer; that is such a work, that a man without the help of the Spirit cannot so much as pray once, much less continue, without it, in a sweet praying frame, and in praying, so to pray as to have his prayers ascend into the ears of the Lord God of Sabaoth.

Jacob did not only begin, but held it: "I will not let thee go, unless thou bless me" (Gen 32). So did the rest of the godly (Hosea 12:4). But this could not be without the spirit of prayer. It is through the Spirit that we have access to the Father (Eph 2:18).

The same is a remarkable place in Jude, when he stirreth up the saints by the judgment of God upon the wicked to stand fast, and continue to hold out in the faith of the gospel, as one excellent means thereto, without which he knew they would never be able to do it. Saith he, "Building up yourselves on your most holy faith, praying in the Holy Ghost" (Jude 20). As if he had said, Brethren, as eternal life is laid up for the persons that hold out only, so you cannot hold out unless you continue praying in the Spirit. The great cheat that the devil and antichrist delude the world withal, it is to make them continue in the form of any duty, the form of preaching, of hearing, or praying, &c. These are they that have "a form of godliness, but denying the power thereof; from such turn away" (2 Tim 3:5).

Here followeth the third thing; to wit,

WHAT IT IS TO PRAY WITH THE SPIRIT, AND WITH THE UNDERSTANDING

THIRD. And now to the next thing, what it is to pray with the Spirit, and to pray with the understanding also. For the apostle puts a clear distinction between praying with the Spirit, and praying with the Spirit and understanding: therefore when he saith, "he will pray with the Spirit," he adds, "and I will pray with the understanding *also*." This distinction was occasioned through the Corinthians not observing that it was their duty to do what they did to the edification of themselves and others too: whereas they did it for their own commendations. So I judge: for many of them having extraordinary gifts, as to speak with divers tongues, &c., therefore they were more for those mighty gifts than they were for the edifying of their brethren; which was the cause that Paul wrote this chapter to them, to let them understand, that though extraordinary gifts were excellent, yet to do what they did to the edification of the church was more excellent. For, saith the apostle, "if I pray in an unknown tongue, my spirit prayeth, but my understanding," and also the understanding of others, "is unfruitful" (1 Cor 14:3, 4, 12, 19, 24, 25. Read the scope of the whole chapter). Therefore, "I will pray with the Spirit, and I will pray with the understanding also."

It is expedient then that the understanding should be occupied in prayer, as well as the heart and mouth: "I will pray with the Spirit, and I will pray with the understanding also." That which is done with understanding, is done more effectually, sensibly, and heartily, as I shall show farther anon, than that which is done without it; which made the apostle pray for the Colossians, that God would fill them "with the knowledge of his will, in all wisdom and spiritual understanding" (Col 1:9). And for the Ephesians, that God would give unto them "the spirit of wisdom and revelation, in the knowledge of him" (Eph 1:17). And so for the Philippians, that God would make them abound "in knowledge, and in all judgment" (Phil 1:9). A suitable understanding is good in everything a man undertakes, either civil or spiritual; and therefore it must be desired by all them that would be a praying people. In my speaking to this, I shall show you what it is to pray with understanding.

Understanding is to be taken both for speaking in our mother- tongue, and also experimentally. I pass the first, and treat only on the second.

For the making of right prayers, it is to be required that there should be a good or spiritual understanding in all them who pray to God.

First. To pray with understanding, is to pray as being instructed by the Spirit in the understanding of the want of those things which the soul is to pray for. Though a man be in never so much need of pardon of sin, and deliverance from wrath to come, yet if he understand not this, he will either not desire them at all, or else be so cold and lukewarm in his desires after them, that God will even loathe his frame of spirit in asking for them. Thus it was with the church of the Laodiceans, they wanted knowledge or spiritual understanding; they knew not that they were poor, wretched, blind, and naked. The cause whereof made them, and all their services, so loathsome to Christ, that he threatens to spew them out of his mouth (Rev 3:16, 17). Men without understanding may say the same words in prayer as others do; but if there be an understanding in the one, and none in the other, there is, O there is a mighty difference in speaking the very same words! The one speaking from a spiritual understanding of those things that he in words desires, and the other words it only, and there is all.

Second. Spiritual understanding espieth in the heart of God a readiness and willingness to give those things to the soul that it stands in need of. David by this could guess at the very thoughts of God towards him (Psa 40:5). And thus it was with the woman of Canaan; she did by faith and a right understanding discern, beyond all the rough carriage of Christ, tenderness and willingness in his heart to save, which caused her to be vehement and earnest, yea, restless, until she did enjoy the mercy she stood in need of (Matt 15:22-28).

And understanding of the willingness that is in the heart of God to save sinners, there is nothing will press the soul more to seek after God, and to cry for pardon, than it. If a man should see a pearl worth an hundred pounds lie in a ditch, yet if he understood not the value of it, he would lightly pass it by: but if he once get the knowledge of it, he would venture up to the neck for it. So it is with souls concerning the things of God: if a man once get an understanding of the worth of them, then his heart, nay, the very strength of his soul, runs after them, and he will never leave crying till he have them. The two blind men in the gospel, because they did certainly know that Jesus, who was going by them, was both able and willing to heal such infirmities as they were afflicted with: therefore they cried, and the more they were rebuked, the more they cried (Matt 20:29- 31).

Third. The understanding being spiritually enlightened, hereby there is the way, as aforesaid, discovered, through which the soul should come unto God; which gives great encouragement unto it. It is else with a poor soul, as with one who hath a work to do, and if it be not done, the danger is great; if it be done, so is the advantage. But he knows not how to begin, nor how to proceed; and so, through discouragement, lets all alone, and runs the hazard.

Fourth. The enlightened understanding sees largeness enough in the promises to encourage it to pray; which still adds to it strength to strength. As when men promise such and such things to all that will come for them, it is great encouragement to those that know what promises are made, to come and ask for them.

Fifth. The understanding being enlightened, way is made for the soul to come to God with suitable arguments, sometimes in a way of expostulation, as Jacob (Gen 32:9). Sometimes in way of supplication, yet not in a verbal way only, but even from the heart there is forced by the Spirit, through the understanding, such effectual arguments as moveth the heart of God. When Ephraim gets a right understanding of his own unseemly carriages towards the Lord, then he begins to bemoan himself (Jer 31:18-20). And in bemoaning of himself, he used such arguments with the Lord, that it affects his heart, draws out forgiveness, and makes Ephraim pleasant in his eyes through Jesus Christ our Lord: "I have surely heard Ephraim bemoaning himself thus," saith God, "Thou hast chastised me, and I was chastised; as a bullock unaccustomed to the yoke; turn thou me, and I shall be turned; for thou art the Lord my God. Surely after that I was turned, I repented, and after that I was instructed," or had a right understanding of myself, "I smote upon my thigh, I was ashamed; yea, even confounded; because I did bear the reproach of my youth." These be Ephraim's complaints and bemoanings of himself; at which the Lord breaks forth into these heart-melting expressions, saying, "Is Ephraim my dear son? Is he a pleasant child? For since I spake against him, I do earnestly remember him still; therefore my bowels are troubled for him; I will surely have mercy upon him, saith the Lord." Thus, you see, that as it is required to pray with the Spirit, so it is to pray with the understanding also. And to illustrate what hath been spoken by a similitude:–set the case, there should come two a-begging to your door; the one is a poor, lame, wounded, and almost starved creature, the other is a healthful lusty person; these two use the same words in their begging; the one saith he is almost starved, so doth the other: but yet the man that is indeed the poor, lame, or maimed person, he speaks with more sense, feeling, and understanding of the misery that is mentioned in their begging, than the other can do; and it is discovered more by his affectionate speaking, his bemoaning himself. His pain and poverty make him speak more in a spirit of lamentation than the other, and he shall be pitied sooner than the other, by all those that have the least dram of natural affection or pity. Just thus it is with God: there are some who out of custom and formality go and pray; there are others who go in the bitterness of their spirits: the one he prays out of bare notion and naked knowledge; the other hath his words forced from him by the anguish of his soul. Surely that is the man that God will look at, "even to him that is poor," of an humble "and of a contrite spirit, and trembleth at my word" (Isa 66:2).

Sixth. An understanding well enlightened is of admirable use also, both as to the matter and manner of prayer. He that hath his understanding well exercised, to discern between good and evil, and in it placed a sense either of the misery of man, or the mercy of God; that soul hath no need of the writings of other men to teach him by forms of prayer. For as he that feels the pain needs not to be taught to cry O! even so he that hath his understanding opened by the Spirit needs not so to be taught of other men's prayers, as that he cannot pray without them. The present sense, feeling, and pressure that lieth upon his spirit, provokes him to groan out his request unto the Lord. When David had the pains of hell catching hold on him, and the sorrows of hell compassing him about, he needs not a bishop in a surplice to teach him to say, "O Lord, I beseech thee, deliver my soul" (Psa 116:3, 4). Or to look into a book, to teach him in a form to pour out his heart before God. It is the nature of the heart of sick men, in their pain and sickness, to vent itself for ease, by dolorous groans and complainings to them that stand by. Thus it was with David, in Psalm 38:1-12. And thus, blessed be the Lord, it is with them that are endued with the grace of God.

Seventh. It is necessary that there be an enlightened understanding, to the end that the soul be kept in a continuation of the duty of prayer.

The people of God are not ignorant how many wiles, tricks, and temptations the devil hath to make a poor soul, who is truly willing to have the Lord Jesus Christ, and that upon Christ's terms too; I say, to tempt that soul to be weary of seeking the face of God, and to think that God is not willing to have mercy on such a one as him. Ay, saith Satan, thou mayest pray indeed, but thou shalt not prevail. Thou seest thine heart is hard, cold, dull, and dread; thou dost not pray with the Spirit, thou dost not pray in good earnest, thy thoughts are running after other things, when thou pretendest to pray to God. Away hypocrite, go no further, it is but in vain to strive any longer! Here now, if the soul be not well informed in its understanding, it will presently cry out, "the Lord hath forsaken me, and my Lord hath forgotten me" (Isa 49:14). Whereas the soul rightly informed and enlightened saith, Well, I will seek the Lord, and wait; I will not leave off, though the Lord keep silence, and speak not one word of comfort (Isa 40:27). He loved Jacob dearly, and yet he made him wrestle before he had the blessing (Gen 32:25-27). Seeming delays in God are no tokens of his displeasure; he may hide his face from his dearest saints (Isa 8:17). He loves to keep his people praying, and to find them ever knocking at the gate of heaven; it may be, says the soul, the Lord tries me, or he loves to hear me groan out my condition before him.

The woman of Canaan would not take seeming denials for real ones; she knew the Lord was gracious, and the Lord will avenge his people, though he bear long with them (Luke 18:1-6). The Lord hath waited longer upon me than I have waited upon him; and thus it was with David, "I waited patiently," saith he; that is, it was long before the Lord answered me, though at the last "he inclined" his ear "unto me, and heard my cry" (Psa 40:1). And the most excellent remedy for this is, an understanding well informed and enlightened. Alas, how many poor souls are there in the world, that truly fear the Lord, who, because they are not well informed in their understanding, are oft ready to give up all for lost, upon almost every trick and temptation of Satan! The Lord pity them, and help them to "pray with the Spirit, and with the understanding also." Much of mine own experience could I here discover; when I have been in my fits of agony of spirit, I have been strongly persuaded to leave off, and to seek the Lord no longer;[10] but being made to understand what great sinners the Lord hath had mercy upon, and how large his promises were still to sinners; and that it was not the whole, but the sick, not the righteous, but the sinner, not the full, but the empty, that he extended his grace and mercy unto. This made me, through the assistance of his Holy Spirit, to cleave to him, to hang upon him, and yet to cry, though for the present he made no answer; and the Lord help all his poor, tempted, and afflicted people to do the like, and to continue, though it be long, according to the saying of the prophet (Hab 2:3). And to help them (to that end) to pray, not by the inventions of men, and their stinted forms, but "with the Spirit, and with the understanding also."

Queries and Objections answered.

And now to answer a query or two, and so to pass on to the next thing.

Query First. But what would you have us poor creatures to do that cannot tell how to pray? The Lord knows I know not either how to pray, or what to pray for.

Answ. Poor heart! thou canst not, thou complainest, pray. Canst thou see thy misery? Hath God showed thee that thou art by nature under the curse of his law? If so, do not mistake, I know thou dost groan and that most bitterly. I am persuaded thou canst scarcely be found doing any thing in thy calling, but prayer breaketh from thy heart. Have not thy groans gone up to heaven from every corner of thy house? (Rom 8:26). I know it is thus; and so also doth thine own sorrowful heart witness thy tears, thy forgetfulness of thy calling, &c. Is not thy heart so full of desires after the things of another world, that many times thou dost even forget the things of this world? Prithee read this scripture, Job 23:12.

Query Second. Yea, but when I go into secret, and intend to pour out my soul before God, I can scarce say anything at all.

Answ. 1. Ah! Sweet soul! It is not thy words that God so much regards, as that he will not mind thee, except thou comest before him with some eloquent oration. His eye is on the brokenness of thine heart; and that it is that makes the very bowels of the Lord to run over. "A broken and a contrite heart, O God, thou wilt not despise" (Psa 51:17).

2. The stopping of thy words may arise from overmuch trouble in thy heart. David was so troubled sometimes, that he could not speak (Psa 77:3, 4). But this may comfort all such sorrowful hearts as thou art, that though thou canst not through the anguish of thy spirit speak much, yet the Holy Spirit stirs up in thine heart groans and sighs, so much the more vehement: when the mouth is hindered, yet the spirit is not. Moses, as aforesaid, made

heaven ring again with his prayers, when (that we read of) not one word came out of his mouth (Exo 14:15). But,

3. If thou wouldst more fully express thyself before the Lord, study, first, Thy filthy estate; secondly, God's promises; thirdly, The heart of Christ. Which thou mayest know or discern, (1.) By his condescension and bloodshed. (2.) By the mercy he hath extended to great sinners formerly, and plead thine own vileness, by way of bemoaning; Christ's blood by way of expostulation; and in thy prayers, let the mercy that he hath extended to other great sinners, together with his rich promises of grace, be much upon thy heart. Yet let me counsel thee, (a.) Take heed that thou content not thyself with words. (b.) That thou do not think that God looks only at them neither. But, (c.) However, whether thy words be few or many, let thine heart go with them; and then shalt thou seek him, and find him, when thou shalt seek him with thy whole heart (Jer 29:13).

Objection. But though you have seemed to speak against any other way of praying but by the Spirit, yet here you yourself can give direction how to pray.

Answ. We ought to prompt one another forward to prayer, though we ought not to make for each other forms of prayer. To exhort to pray with Christian direction is one thing, and to make stinted forms for the tying up the Spirit of God to them is another thing. The apostle gives them no form to pray withal, yet directs to prayer (Eph 6:18; Rom 15:30-32). Let no man therefore conclude, that because we may with allowance give instructions and directions to pray, that therefore it is lawful to make for each other forms of prayer.

Object. But if we do not use forms of prayer, how shall we teach our children to pray?

Answ. My judgment is, that men go the wrong way to teach their children to pray, in going about so soon to teach them any set company of words, as is the common use of poor creatures to do.

For to me it seems to be a better way for people betimes to tell their children what cursed creatures they are, and how they are under the wrath of God by reason of original and actual sin; also to tell them the nature of God's wrath, and the duration of the misery; which if they conscientiously do, they would sooner teach their children to pray than they do. The way that men learn to pray, it is by conviction for sin; and this is the way to make our sweet babes do so too. But the other way, namely, to be busy in teaching children forms of prayer, before they know any thing else, it is the next way to make them cursed hypocrites, and to puff them up with pride. Teach therefore your children to know their wretched state and condition; tell them of hell-fire and their sins, of damnation, and salvation; the way to escape the one, and to enjoy the other, if you know it yourselves, and this will make tears run down your sweet babes' eyes, and hearty groans flow from their hearts; and then also you may tell them to whom they should pray, and through whom they should pray: you may tell them also of God's promises, and his former grace extended to sinners, according to the word.

Ah! Poor sweet babes, the Lord open their eyes, and make them holy Christians. Saith David, "Come ye children, hearken unto me; I will teach you the fear of the Lord" (Psa 34:11). He doth not say, I will muzzle you up in a form of prayer; but "I will teach you the fear of the Lord"; which is, to see their sad states by nature, and to be instructed in the truth of the gospel, which doth through the Spirit beget prayer in every one that in truth learns it. And the more you teach them this, the more will their hearts run out to God in prayer. God never did account Paul a praying man, until he was a convinced and converted man; no more will it be with any else (Acts 9:11).

Object. But we find that the disciples desired that Christ would teach them to pray, as John also taught his disciples; and that thereupon he taught them that form called the LORD'S PRAYER.

Answ. 1. To be taught by Christ, is that which not only they, but we desire; and seeing he is not here in his person to teach us, the Lord teach us by his Word and Spirit; for the Spirit it is which he hath said he would send to supply in his room when he went away, as it is (John 14:16; 16:7).

2. As to that called a form, I cannot think that Christ intended it as a stinted form of prayer. (1.) Because he himself layeth it down diversely, as is to be seen, if you compare Matthew 6 and Luke 11. Whereas if he intended it as a set form, it must not have been so laid down, for a set form is so many words and no more. (2.) We do not find that the apostles did ever observe it as such; neither did they admonish others so to do. Search all their epistles, yet surely they, both for knowledge to discern and faithfulness to practice, were as eminent as any HE ever since in the world which would impose it.

[3.] But, in a word, Christ by those words, "Our Father," &c., doth instruct his people what rules they should observe in their prayers to God. (1.) That they should pray in faith. (2.) To God in the heavens. (3.) For such things as are according to his will, &c. Pray thus, or after this manner.

Object. But Christ bids pray for the Spirit; this implieth that men without the Spirit may notwithstanding pray and be heard. (See Luke 11:9-13).

Answ. The speech of Christ there is directed to his own (verse 1). Christ's telling of them that God would give his Holy Spirit to them that ask him, is to be understood of giving more of the Holy Spirit; for still they are the disciples spoken to, which had a measure of the Spirit already; for he saith, "when ye pray, say, Our Father," (verse 2) I say unto you (verse 8). And I say unto you, (verse 9) "If ye then, being evil, know how to give good gifts unto your children, how much more shall your heavenly Father give the Holy Spirit to them that ask him," (verse 13). Christians ought to pray for the Spirit, that is, for more of it, though God hath endued them with it already.

Quest. Then would you have none pray but those that know they are the disciples of Christ?

Answ. Yes.

1. Let every soul that would be saved pour out itself to God, though it cannot through temptation conclude itself a child of God. And,

2. I know if the grace of God be in thee, it will be as natural to

thee to groan out thy condition, as it is for a sucking child to cry for the breast. Prayer is one of the first things that discovers a man to be a Christian (Acts 9:12). But yet if it be right, it is such prayer as followeth. (1.) To desire God in Christ, for himself, for his holiness, love, wisdom, and glory. For right prayer, as it runs only to God through Christ, so it centers in him, and in him alone. "Whom have I in heaven but thee? And there is none upon earth that I desire," long for, or seek after, "beside thee" (Psa 73:25). (2.) That the soul might enjoy continually communion with him, both here and hereafter. "I shall be satisfied, when I awake with" thine image, or in "thy likeness," (Psa 17:15). "For in this we groan earnestly," &c., (2 Cor 5:2). (3.) Right prayer is accompanied with a continual labour after that which is prayed for. "My soul waiteth for the Lord more than they that watch for the morning" (Psa 130:6). "I will rise now, I will seek him whom my soul loveth" (Song 3:2). For mark, I beseech you, there are two things that provoke to prayer. The one is a detestation to sin, and the things of this life; the other is a longing desire after communion with God, in a holy and undefiled state and inheritance. Compare but this one thing with most of the prayers that are made by men, and you shall find them but mock prayers, and the breathings of an abominable spirit; for even the most of men either do pray at all, or else only endeavour to mock God and the world by so doing; for do but compare their prayer and the course of their lives together, and you may easily see that the thing included in their prayer is the least looked after by their lives. O sad hypocrites!

Thus have I briefly showed you, FIRST, What prayer is; SECOND, What it is to pray with the Spirit; THIRD, What it is to pray with the Spirit, and with the understanding also.

FOURTH. USE AND APPLICATION

I shall now speak a word or two of application, and so conclude with, First, A word of information; Second, A word of encouragement; Third, A word of rebuke.

USE First, A word of information.

For the first to inform you; as prayer is the duty of every one of the children of God, and carried on by the Spirit of Christ in the soul; so every one that doth but offer to take upon him to pray to the Lord, had need be very wary, and go about that work especially with the dread of God, as well as with hopes of the mercy of God through Jesus Christ.

Prayer is an ordinance of God, in which a man draws very near to God; and therefore it calleth for so much the more of the assistance of the grace of God to help a soul to pray as becomes one that is in the presence of him. It is a shame for a man to behave himself irreverently before a king, but a sin to do so before God. And as a king, if wise, is not pleased with an oration made up with unseemly words and gestures, so God takes no pleasure in the sacrifice of fools (Eccl 5:1, 4). It is not long discourses, nor eloquent tongues, that are the things which are pleasing in the ears of the Lord; but a humble, broken, and contrite heart, that is sweet in the nostrils of the heavenly Majesty (Psa 51:17; Isa 57:15). Therefore for information, know that there are these five things that are obstructions to prayer, and even make void the requests of the creature.

1. When men regard iniquity in their hearts, at the time of their prayers before God. "If I regard iniquity in my heart, the Lord will not hear" my prayer (Psa 66:18). For the preventing of temptation, that by the misunderstanding of this may seize thy heart, when there is a secret love to that very thing which thou

with thy dissembling lips dost ask for strength against. For this is the wickedness of man's heart, that it will even love, and hold fast, that which with the mouth it prays against: and of this sort are they that honour God with their mouth, but their heart is far from him (Isa 29:13; Eze 33:31). O! how ugly would it be in our eyes, if we should see a beggar ask an alms, with an intention to throw it to the dogs! Or that should say with one breath, Pray, you bestow this upon me; and with the next, I beseech you, give it me not! And yet thus it is with these kind of persons; with their mouth they say, "Thy will be done"; and with their hearts nothing less. With their mouth say, "Hallowed be thy name"; and with their hearts and lives thy delight to dishonour him all the day long. These be the prayers that become sin (Psa 109:7), and though they put them up often, yet the Lord will never answer them (2 Sam 22:42).

2. When men pray for a show to be heard, and thought somebody in religion, and the like; these prayers also fall far short of God's approbation, and are never like to be answered, in reference to eternal life. There are two sorts of men that pray to this end.

(1.) Your trencher chaplains, that thrust themselves into great men's families, pretending the worship of God, when in truth the great business is their own bellies; and were notably painted out by Ahab's prophets, and also Nebuchadnezzar's wise men, who, though they pretended great devotion, yet their lusts and their bellies were the great things aimed at by them in all their pieces of devotion.

(2.) Them also that seek repute and applause for their eloquent terms, and seek more to tickle the ears and heads of their hearers than anything else. These be they that pray to be heard of men, and have all their reward already (Matt 6:5). These persons are discovered thus, (a.) They eye only their auditory in their expressions. (b.) They look for commendation when they have done. (c.) Their hearts either rise or fall according to their praise or enlargement. (d.) The length of their prayer pleaseth them; and that it might be long, they will vainly repeat things over and over (Matt 6:7). They study for enlargements, but look not from what heart they come; they look for returns, but it is the windy applause of men. And therefore they love not to be in their chamber, but among company: and if at any time conscience thrusts them into their closet, yet hypocrisy will cause them to be heard in the streets; and when their mouths have done going their prayers are ended; for they wait not to hearken what the Lord will say (Psa 85:8).

3. A third sort of prayer that will not be accepted of God, it is, when either they pray for wrong things, or if for right things, yet that the thing prayed for might be spent upon their lusts, and laid out to wrong ends. Some have not, because they ask not, saith James, and others ask and have not, because they ask amiss, that they may consume it on their lusts (James 4: 2-4). Ends contrary to God's will is a great argument with God to frustrate the petitions presented before him. Hence it is that so many pray for this and that, and yet receive it not. God answers them only with silence; they have their words for their labour; and that is all. Object. But God hears some persons, though their hearts be not right with him, as he did Israel, in giving quails, though they spent them upon their lusts (Psa 106:14). Answ. If he doth, it is in judgment, not in mercy. He gave them their desire indeed, but they had better have been without it, for he "sent leanness into their soul" (Psa 106:15). Woe be to that man that God answereth thus.

4. Another sort of prayers there are that are not answered; and those are such as are made by men, and presented to God in their own persons only, without their appearing in the Lord Jesus. For though God hath appointed prayer, and promised to hear the prayer of the creature, yet not the prayer of any creature that comes not in Christ. "If ye shall ask anything in my name." And whether ye eat or drink, or whatsoever ye do, do all in the name of the Lord Jesus Christ (Col 3:17). "If ye shall ask anything in my name," &c., (John 14:13, 14), though you be never so devout, zealous, earnest and constant in prayer, yet it is in Christ only that you must be heard and accepted. But, alas! the most of men know not what it is to come to him in the name of the Lord Jesus, which is the reason they either live wicked, pray wicked, and also die wicked. Or else, that they attain to nothing else but what a mere natural man may attain unto, as to be exact in word

and deed betwixt man and man, and only with the righteousness of the law to appear before God.

5. The last thing that hindereth prayer is, the form of it without the power. It is an easy thing for men to be very hot for such things as forms of prayer, as they are written in a book; but yet they are altogether forgetful to inquire with themselves, whether they have the spirit and power of prayer. These men are like a painted man, and their prayers like a false voice. They in person appear as hypocrites, and their prayers are an abomination (Prov 28:9). When they say they have been pouring out their souls to God he saith they have been howling like dogs (Hosea 7:14).

When therefore thou intendest, or art minded to pray to the Lord of heaven and earth, consider these following particulars. 1. Consider seriously what thou wantest. Do not, as many who in their words only beat the air, and ask for such things as indeed they do not desire, nor see that they stand in need thereof. 2. When thou seest what thou wantest, keep to that, and take heed thou pray sensibly.

Object. But I have a sense of nothing; then, by your argument, I must not pray at all.

Answ. 1. If thou findest thyself senseless in some sad measure, yet thou canst not complain of that senselessness, but by being sensible there is a sense of senselessness. According to thy sense, then, that thou hast of the need of anything, so pray; (Luke 8:9), and if thou art sensible of thy senselessness, pray the Lord to make thee sensible of whatever thou findest thine heart senseless of. This was the usual practice of the holy men of God. "Lord, make me to know mine end," saith David (Psa 39:4). "Lord, open to us this parable," said the disciples (Luke 8:9). And to this is annexed the promise, "Call unto me and I will answer thee, and show thee great and mighty things which thou knowest not," that thou art not sensible of (Jer 33:3). But,

Answ. 2. Take heed that thy heart go to God as well as thy mouth. Let not thy mouth go any further than thou strivest to draw thine heart along with it. David would lift his heart and soul to the Lord; and good reason; for so far as a man's mouth goeth along without his heart, so far it is but lip-labour only; and though God calls for, and accepteth the calves of the lips, yet the lips without the heart argueth, not only senselessness, but our being without sense of our senselessness; and therefore if thou hast a mind to enlarge in prayer before God, see that it be with thy heart.

Answ. 3. Take heed of affecting expressions, and so to please thyself with the use of them, that thou forget not the life of prayer.

I shall conclude this use with a caution or two.

Caution 1. And the first is, take heed thou do not throw off prayer, through sudden persuasions that thou hast not the Spirit, neither prayest thereby. It is the great work of the devil to do his best, or rather worst, against the best prayers. He will flatter your false dissembling hypocrites, and feed them with a thousand fancies of well-doing, when their very duties of prayer, and all other, stink in the nostrils of God, when he stands at a poor Joshua's hand to resist him, that is, to persuade him, that neither his person nor performances are accepted of God (Isa 65:5; Zech 3:1). Take heed, therefore, of such false conclusions and groundless discouragements; and though such persuasions do come in upon thy spirit, be so far from being discouraged by them, that thou use them to put thee upon further sincerity and restlessness of spirit, in thy approaching to God.

Caution 2. As such sudden temptations should not stop thee from prayer, and pouring out thy soul to God; so neither should thine own heart's corruptions hinder thee. (Let not thy corruptions stop thy prayers). It may be thou mayest find in thee all those things before mentioned, and that they will be endeavouring to put forth themselves in thy praying to him. Thy business then is to judge them, to pray against them, and to lay thyself so much the more at the foot of God, in a sense of thy own vileness, and rather make an argument from thy vileness and corruption of heart, to plead with God for justifying and sanctifying grace, than an argument of discouragement and despair. David went this way. "O Lord," saith he, "pardon mine iniquity, for it is great" (Psa 25:11).

USE Second. A word of encouragement.

And therefore, secondly, to speak a word by way of encouragement, to the poor, tempted, and cast down soul, to pray to God through Christ. Though all prayer that is accepted of God in reference to eternal life must be in the Spirit–for that only maketh intercession for us according to the will of God, (Rom 8:27)–yet because many poor souls may have the Holy Spirit working on them, and stirring of them to groan unto the Lord for mercy, though through unbelief they do not, nor, for the present, cannot believe that they are the people of God, such as he delights in; yet forasmuch as the truth of grace may be in them, therefore I shall, to encourage them, lay down further these few particulars.

1. That scripture in Luke 11:8 is very encouraging to any poor soul that doth hunger after Christ Jesus. In verses 5-7, he speaketh a parable of a man that went to his friend to borrow three loaves, who, because he was in bed, denied him; yet for his importunity-sake, he did arise and give him, clearly signifying that though poor souls, through the weakness of their faith, cannot see that they are the friends of God, yet they should never leave asking, seeking, and knocking at God's door for mercy. Mark, saith Christ, "I say unto you, though he will not rise and give him, because he is his friend; yet because of his importunity," or restless desires, "he will rise and give him as many as he needeth." Poor heart! thou criest out that God will not regard thee, thou dost not find that thou art a friend to him, but rather an enemy in thine heart by wicked works (Col 1:21). And thou art as though thou didst hear the Lord saying to thee, Trouble me not, I cannot give unto thee, as he in the parable; yet I say, continue knocking, crying, moaning, and bewailing thyself. I tell thee, "though he will not rise and give thee, because thou art his friend; yet, because of thy importunity, he will arise and give thee as many as thou needest." The same in effect you have discovered, Luke 18, in the parable of the unjust judge and the poor widow; her importunity prevailed with him. And verily, mine own experience tells me, that there is nothing that doth more prevail with God than importunity. Is it not so with you in respect of your beggars that come to your door? Though you have no heart to give them anything at their first asking, yet if they follow you,

bemoaning themselves, and will take no nay without an alms, you will give them; for their continual begging overcometh you. Are there bowels in you that are wicked, and will they be wrought upon by an importuning beggar? Go thou and do the like. It is a prevailing motive, and that by good experience, he will arise and give thee as many as thou needest (Luke 11:8).

2. Another encouragement for a poor trembling convinced soul is to consider the place, throne, or seat, on which the great God hath placed himself to hear the petitions and prayers of poor creatures; and that is a "throne of grace" (Heb 4:16). "The mercy-seat" (Exo 25:22). Which signifieth that in the days of the gospel God hath taken up his seat, his abiding-place, in mercy and forgiveness; and from thence he doth intend to hear the sinner, and to commune with him, as he saith (Exo 25:22),–speaking before of the mercy-seat–"And there I will meet with thee," mark, it is upon the mercy-seat: "There I will meet with thee, and" there "I will commune with thee, from above the mercy-seat." Poor souls! They are very apt to entertain strange thoughts of God, and his carriage towards them: and suddenly to conclude that God will have no regard unto them, when yet he is upon the mercy-seat, and hath taken up his place on purpose there, to the end he may hear and regard the prayers of poor creatures. If he had said, I will commune with thee from my throne of judgment, then indeed you might have trembled and fled from the face of the great and glorious Majesty. But when he saith he will hear and commune with souls upon the throne of grace, or from the mercy-seat, this should encourage thee, and cause thee to hope, nay, to "come boldly unto the throne of grace, that thou mayest obtain mercy, and find grace to help in time of need" (Heb 4:16).

3. There is yet another encouragement to continue in prayer with God: and that is this:

As there is a mercy seat, from whence God is willing to commune with poor sinners; so there is also by his mercy-seat, Jesus Christ, who continually besprinkleth it with his blood. Hence it is called "the blood of sprinkling" (Heb 12:24). When the high-priest under the law was to go into the holiest, where the mercy-seat was, he might not go in "without blood" (Heb 9:7).

Why so? Because, though God was upon the mercy-seat, yet he was perfectly just as well as merciful. Now the blood was to stop justice from running out upon the persons concerned in the intercession of the high-priest, as in Leviticus 16:13-17, to signify that all thine unworthiness that thou fearest should not hinder thee from coming to God in Christ for mercy. Thou criest out that thou art vile, and therefore God will not regard thy prayers; it is true, if thou delight in thy vileness, and come to God out of a mere pretence. But if from a sense of thy vileness thou do pour out thy heart to God, desiring to be saved from the guilt, and cleansed from the filth, with all thy heart; fear not, thy vileness will not cause the Lord to stop his ear from hearing of thee. The value of the blood of Christ which is sprinkled upon the mercy-seat stops the course of justice, and opens a floodgate for the mercy of the Lord to be extended unto thee. Thou hast therefore, as aforesaid, "boldness to enter into the holiest by the blood of Jesus," that hath made "a new and living way" for thee, thou shalt not die (Heb 10:19, 20).

Besides, Jesus is there, not only to sprinkle the mercy-seat with his blood, but he speaks, and his blood speaks; he hath audience, and his blood hath audience; insomuch that God saith, when he doth but see the blood, he "will pass over you, and the plague shall not be upon you," &c., (Exo 12:13).

I shall not detain you any longer. Be sober and humble; go to the Father in the name of the Son, and tell him your case, in the assistance of the Spirit, and you will then feel the benefit of praying with the Spirit and with the understanding also.

USE Third. A word of reproof.

1. This speaks sadly to you who never pray at all. "I will pray," saith the apostle, and so saith the heart of them that are Christians. Thou then art not a Christian that art not a praying person. The promise is that every one that is righteous shall pray (Psa 32:6). Thou then art a wicked wretch that prayest not. Jacob got the name of Israel by wrestling with God (Gen 32). And all his

children bare that name with him (Gal 6:16). But the people that forget prayer, that call not on the name of the Lord, they have prayer made for them, but it is such as this, "Pour out thy fury upon the heathen," O Lord, "and upon the families that call not on thy name" (Jer 10:25). How likest thou this, O thou that art so far off from pouring out thine heart before God, that thou goest to bed like a dog, and risest like a hog, or a sot, and forgettest to call upon God? What wilt thou do when thou shalt be damned in hell, because thou couldst not find in thine heart to ask for heaven? Who will grieve for thy sorrow, that didst not count mercy worth asking for? I tell thee, the ravens, the dogs, &c., shall rise up in judgment against thee, for they will, according to their kind, make signs, and a noise for something to refresh them when they want it; but thou hast not the heart to ask for heaven, though thou must eternally perish in hell, if thou hast it not.

2. This rebukes you that make it your business to slight, mock at, and undervalue the Spirit, and praying by that. What will you do, when God shall come to reckon for these things? You count it high treason to speak but a word against the king, nay, you tremble at the thought of it; and yet in the meantime you will blaspheme the Spirit of the Lord. Is God indeed to be dallied with, and will the end be pleasant unto you? Did God send his Holy Spirit into the hearts of his people, to that end that you should taunt at it? Is this to serve God? And doth this demonstrate the reformation of your church? Nay, is it not the mark of implacable reprobates? O fearful! Can you not be content to be damned for your sins against the law, but you must sin against the Holy Ghost?

Must the holy, harmless, and undefiled Spirit of grace, the nature of God, the promise of Christ, the Comforter of his children, that without which no man can do any service acceptable to the Father–must this, I say, be the burthen of your song, to taunt, deride, and mock at? If God sent Korah and his company headlong to hell for speaking against Moses and Aaron, do you that mock at the Spirit of Christ think to escape unpunished? (Num 16; Heb 10:29). Did you never read what God did to Ananias and Sapphira for telling but one lie against it? (Acts 5:1-8). Also to

Simon Magus for but undervaluing of it? (Acts 8:18-22). And will thy sin be a virtue, or go unrewarded with vengeance, that makest it thy business to rage against, and oppose its office, service, and help, that it giveth unto the children of God? It is a fearful thing to do despite unto the Spirit of grace (Compare Matt 12:31, with Mark 3:28-30).

3. As this is the doom of those who do openly blaspheme the Holy Ghost, in a way of disdain and reproach to its office and service: so also it is sad for you, who resist the Spirit of prayer, by a form of man's inventing. A very juggle of the devil, that the traditions of men should be of better esteem, and more to be owned than the Spirit of prayer. What is this less than that accursed abomination of Jeroboam, which kept many from going to Jerusalem, the place and way of God's appointment to worship; and by that means brought such displeasure from God upon them, as to this day is not appeased? (1 Kings 12:26-33). One would think that God's judgments of old upon the hypocrites of that day should make them that have heard of such things take heed and fear to do so. Yet the doctors of our day are so far from taking of warning by the punishment of others, that they do most desperately rush into the same transgression, viz., to set up an institution of man, neither commanded nor commended of God; and whosoever will not obey herein, they must be driven either out of the land or the world.

Hath God required these things at your hands? If he hath, show us where? If not, as I am sure he hath not, then what cursed presumption is it in any pope, bishop, or other, to command that in the worship of God which he hath not required? Nay further, it is not that part only of the form, which is several texts of Scripture that we are commanded to say, but even all must be confessed as the divine worship of God, notwithstanding those absurdities contained therein, which because they are at large discovered by others, I omit the rehearsal of them. Again, though a man be willing to live never so peaceably, yet because he cannot, for conscience sake, own that for one of the most eminent parts of God's worship, which he never commanded, therefore must that man be looked upon as factious, seditious, erroneous, heretical–a disparagement to the church, a seducer of the people, and what not? Lord, what will be the fruit of these things, when for the doctrine of God there is imposed, that is, more than taught, the traditions of men? Thus is the Spirit of prayer disowned, and the form imposed; the Spirit debased, and the form extolled; they that pray with the Spirit, though never so humble and holy, counted fanatics; and they that pray with the form, though with that only, counted the virtuous! And how will the favorers of such a practice answer that Scripture, which commandeth that the church should turn away from such as have "a form of godliness, and deny the power thereof"? (2 Tim 3:5). And if I should say that men that do these things aforesaid, do advance a form of prayer of other men's making, above the spirit of prayer, it would not take long time to prove it. For he that advanceth the book of Common Prayer above the Spirit of prayer, he doth advance a form of men's making above it. But this do all those who banish, or desire to banish, them that pray with the Spirit of prayer; while they hug and embrace them that pray by that form only, and that because they do it. Therefore they love and advance the form of their own or others' inventing, before the Spirit of prayer, which is God's special and gracious appointment.

If you desire the clearing of the minor, look into the jails in England, and into the alehouses of the same; and I trow you will find those that plead for the Spirit of prayer in the jail, and them that look after the form of men's inventions only in the alehouse. It is evident also by the silencing of God's dear ministers, though never so powerfully enabled by the Spirit of prayer, if they in conscience cannot admit of that form of Common Prayer. If this be not an exalting the Common Prayer Book above either praying by the Spirit, or preaching the Word, I have taken my mark amiss. It is not pleasant for me to dwell on this. The Lord in mercy turn the hearts of the people to seek more after the Spirit of prayer; and in the strength of that, to pour out their souls before the Lord. Only let me say it is a sad sign, that that which is one of the most eminent parts of the pretended worship of God is Antichristian, when it hath nothing but the tradition of men, and the strength of persecution, to uphold or plead for it.

THE CONCLUSION

I shall conclude this discourse with this word of advice to all God's people. 1. Believe that as sure as you are in the way of God you must meet with temptations. 2. The first day therefore that thou dost enter into Christ's congregation, look for them. 3. When they do come, beg of God to carry thee through them. 4. Be jealous of thine own heart, that it deceive thee not in thy evidences for heaven, nor in thy walking with God in this world. 5. Take heed of the flatteries of false brethren. 6. Keep in the life and power of truth. 7. Look most at the things which are not seen. 8. Take heed of little sins. 9. Keep the promise warm upon thy heart. 10. Renew thy acts of faith in the blood of Christ. 11. Consider the work of thy generation. 12. Count to run with the foremost therein.

Grace be with thee.

FOOTNOTES

[1] Dr. Watt's Guide to Prayer.

[2] Vol iii., p. 346.

[3] Vol iii., p. 298.

[4] Pilgrimage of Perfection, 4to, 1526, vol. iii., p. 9.

[5] Effectual fervent prayer is wrought in the heart by the Holy Ghost, and those objects for which HE inclines the soul to pray are bestowed by God. Thus great things were obtained by Jacob, (Gen 32:24-28); by Moses, (Exo 30:11-14; Num 14:13- 21); by Joshua, (10:12-14); by Hezekiah, (2 Kings 19:14-37); by the woman of Canaan, (Matt 15:21-28). The effectual fervent prayer of a righteous man availeth much, (James 5:16).

[6] How easy to forget all God's benefits, and how impossible it is to remember them all!

[7] See Mr. Fox's citation of the mass, in the last volume of the Book of Martyrs.

[8] Jesus Christ has opened the way to God the Father, by the sacrifice He made for us upon the cross. The holiness and justice of God need not frighten sinners and keep them back. Only let them cry to God in the name of Jesus, only let them plead the atoning blood of Jesus, and they shall find God upon a throne of grace, willing and ready to hear. The name of Jesus is a never-failing passport to our prayers. In that name a man may draw near to God with boldness, and ask with confidence. God has engaged to hear him. Reader, think of this; is not this encouragement?–J. C. Ryle.

[9] See Mr. Fox's Acts and Monuments, v.2.

[10] "In these days, I should find my heart to shut itself up against the Lord, and against his holy Word: I have found my unbelief to set, as it were, the shoulder to the door to keep him out."– Grace Abounding, No. 81.

Lightning Source UK Ltd.
Milton Keynes UK
UKHW052149071021
391777UK00012BA/2654